Madame Alexander

STORE EXCLUSIVES
&
LIMITED EDITIONS

IDENTIFICATION & VALUES

Linda Crowsey

COLLECTOR BOOKS
A *Division of Schroeder Publishing Co., Inc.*

The current values in this book should be used only as a guide. They are not intended to set prices, which vary from one section of the country to another. Auction prices as well as dealer prices vary greatly and are affected by condition as well as demand. Neither the author nor the publisher assumes responsibility for any losses which might be incurred as a result of consulting this guide.

ON THE COVER:
Top left: *Queen during Investiture*
Top right: *Coronation Ball Dancer*
Bottom left: *M.A.D.C. Diamond Pixie*
Bottom middle: *I. Magnin Bon Voyage Miss Magnin*
Bottom right: *I. Magnin Bon Voyage Little Miss Magnin*

Cover design: *Beth Summers*   Book design: *Sherry Kraus*

Searching For A Publisher?

We are always looking for knowledgeable people considered experts within their fields. If you feel that there is a real need for a book on your collectible subject and have a large comprehensive collection, contact Collector Books.

Collector Books
P.O. Box 3009
Paducah, KY 42002-3009

www.collectorbooks.com

Copyright © 2000 by Linda Crowsey

Contents

Dedication

I dedicate *Madame Alexander Store Exclusives and Limited Editions* to the two women who have deeply touched my life and changed it forever.

To Patricia R. Smith who has brought joy to countless collectors through her books, articles, and seminars. Pat introduced me to Madame Beatrice Alexander and to the publishing world. She is always willing to share her knowledge and help in any way she can.

To Madame Beatrice Alexander whose great talent is exhibited in this book. She set the highest standards for her magnificent creations. Her dolls delight both children and adults. Through her dolls she will live forever.

About the Author

Linda C. Crowsey is the author of *Madame Alexander Collectors Dolls Price Guide* volumes 22, 23, 24, and 25. She began collecting Madame Alexander dolls in 1975, and will celebrate her twenty-fifth year in the Madame Alexander Doll Club in 2000. Ms. Crowsey is a charter member of *Who's Who in MADC* and serves on the MADC board of directors. Ms. Crowsey has given lectures and slide presentations on Madame Alexander dolls. She has written articles for the MADC *Review* and for other publications.

Linda and her husband, Howard, make their home in Texas. They have three children and five grandchildren.

The photo acknowledgments are as follows:
Brooklyn Children's Museum and curator Nancy Paine, Louise Albertson, Pat Burns, Lorraine Brown, Joseph Carrillo, Brenda Gay, Gary Green, Shirley Harwood, Judene Hansen, Susan Huey, Chris Law, Ric Markin, Sherry Moran, Lahanta McIntyre, Christene McWilliams, Jennifer O'Connor, Mary Lou Pendergrass, Kyle Ratcliff, Judy Smith, Dwight and Patricia Smith, Marylee Stallings, Billie Stevens, Turn-of-the-Century Antiques, Joette Winn, and Susan York.

Acknowledgments

Preface

Madame Beatrice Alexander was born on March 9, 1895, in Brooklyn, New York. Her father, Maurice Alexander, owned the first doll hospital in America. Maurice repaired antiques and restored porcelain and bisque dolls. Young Beatrice became aware of the pain experienced by a child when their favorite doll was broken. During World War I no dolls or items were available from Germany, the primary source of bisque dolls. Madame and her three sisters began making cloth dolls to sell in the shop. The first of the dolls is thought to be a Red Cross Nurse to honor the brave women serving in the war.

Beatrice married Phillip Behrman in 1912. Mildred was born to Madame and her husband in 1915. Madame joined with her husband to form the Madame Alexander Doll Company in 1923. The cloth dolls were a success, and by the 1930s Madame was making quality dolls in composition. Madame's desire to make a doll that was not easily broken was accomplished. Madame designed costumes for the dolls that were of the finest materials and the detail on the costumes was unequalled in the industry. There is no doubt that the Alexander Doll Company was built, and survived during difficult economic times, because of Madame's creativity and perseverance. Madame Alexander was awarded the Fashion Academy Gold Medal in 1951, 1952, 1953, and 1954 for the fashions she created for her dolls. Madame has received numerous honors for achievements in the doll world and for her philanthropy during her lifetime.

I met Madame Alexander in 1983 at Disney World. Madame gave a small talk and then answered questions. She told about the beginning of her company and how she could not get financing or sign contracts because she was a woman. Madame said her biggest selling job was convincing her husband to resign from his stable job and join her to form the Alexander Doll Company. She was asked what was her favorite doll? Madame replied, "Does a mother have a favorite child? If she does, does she tell?" Madame and I corresponded until her death in 1990. Madame attended the 1985, 1986, and 1987 Madame Alexander Doll Conventions. I am very thankful that I had the honor to meet and correspond with her. I treasure her letters.

Madame sold the Alexander Doll Company to private investors in 1988. The company sold again in 1995. The Madame Alexander Doll Company celebrated its seventy-fifth anniversary in 1998 and continues to make the most beautiful dolls in the world.

Madame Alexander Limited Editions

The purpose of this book is to concentrate on the limited editions produced by the Madame Alexander Doll Company since 1980. The company made the 8" Enchanted Doll House doll in 1980 which sold out immediately. In 1981 the Madame Alexander Company made the 8" Enchanted Doll House doll again, but changed the material on the pinafore to eyelet. These dolls sold quickly. Thus began the new era of limited edition dolls. The Madame Alexander Doll Company has produced dolls exclusively for certain stores almost from the very beginning of the company. For many years the Madame Alexander Doll Company made exclusives for FAO Schwarz, Wanamakers, Neiman Marcus, Marshall Fields, Disney, etc. Sometimes the special dolls came with wardrobes and trunks. During the period from 1965 to 1980 very few special dolls were made.

Limited edition dolls made by the Madame Alexander Doll Company can be placed in one of four categories — store or event exclusives, mid-year releases, factory altered, or factory re-dressed dolls.

Store or event exclusives are dolls designed exclusively for a store or event. The dolls may be limited in the number produced, the length of time produced, or simply they were made exclusively for that store. These dolls do not appear in the yearly Alexander Doll Company catalogs, but do often appear in the individual store catalogs. Event dolls are designed exclusively for a specific event. Store or event dolls produced in very limited numbers are thought to be more desirable because they have a better opportunity of rising in value. The Madame Alexander Doll Company has made and is continuing to make one-of-a-kind auction and raffle dolls for special events. Some of these dolls are pictured in this book, but because they are one-of-a-kind no prices are shown.

The Madame Alexander Doll Company began in 1991 producing dolls in limited numbers for the mid-year. The dolls are usually available in September. The first mid-year release was the 8" Welcome Home made to honor the servicemen and women returning from Desert Storm. The mid-year releases do not appear in the regular company catalog but are now pictured in a smaller booklet. The mid-year release dolls are limited editions because of their reduced production time of usually six months.

Factory altered dolls (F.A.D.) are made in a limited edition for a store or event. A doll from the regular Alexander line is altered by adding accessories such as a hat, scarf, jacket, coat, etc. Often the added item is tagged with the new event name.

A factory re-dressed doll begins with a doll from the Alexander regular line. A completely original outfit is designed and tagged for the store or event. The doll from the regular line is undressed and re-dressed in her completely original outfit. The doll is placed in a new box with the event or store name on it. Often the old outfit from the regular line is included in the new box with the doll and her new outfit.

1953 Coronation Set

In 1952 Madame Alexander was approached by Abraham and Straus, a large Brooklyn department store, to make a set of dolls depicting the Coronation of Queen Elizabeth II. Madame Alexander made the set of 36 dolls that were displayed by Abraham and Straus in an elaborate setting appropriate for the coronation. Madame Alexander researched the clothing, fabrics, jewelry, and crowns. The detail on the set is almost unbelievable. The set was on display during the Coronation of Queen Elizabeth II and was shown on TV by CBS. The set of dolls were later donated to the Brooklyn Children's Museum. My deepest thanks to Ms. Nancy Paine, curator, and to the Brooklyn Children's Museum for giving permission for me to photograph and share this one-of-a-kind magnificent coronation set with collectors.

Coronation Ball Dancer, 18" (Margaret). Her beautiful ball gown is embroidered in gold. She wears a gold necklace, earrings, and tiara.

Coronation Ball Dancer, 18" (Maggie). Her purple velvet ball gown has a sash across the front. She wears an array of diamond jewelry.

Coronation Ball Dancer, 18" (Margaret). Her pink ballgown is embroidered with gold and jewels. She wears a gold tiara of rubies and three bracelets.

Coronation Ball Dancer, 18" (Maggie). This gown has a striped panel down the side. A diamond and star sash drapes across the gown. She wears a diamond tiara.

Coronation Ball Dancer, 18" (Winnie). Her black velvet gown is decorated with sequins to form a leaf design. She wears two bracelets, gold earrings, and tiara.

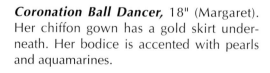

Coronation Ball Dancer, 18" (Margaret). Her chiffon gown has a gold skirt underneath. Her bodice is accented with pearls and aquamarines.

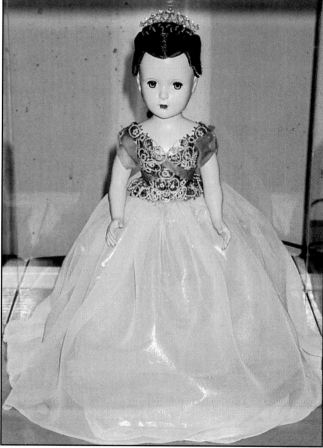

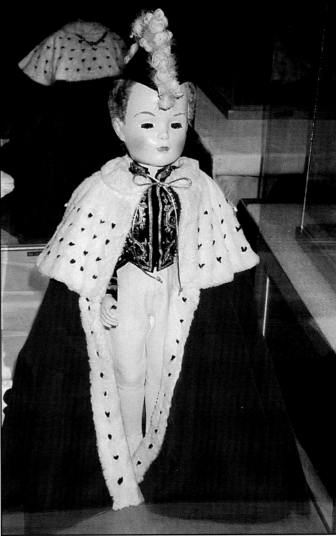

Privy Councillor's Lady, 18" (Margaret). She wears a lace gown decorated with diamonds under a red velvet layered robe. She carries a red velvet bag trimmed in gold.

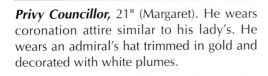

Privy Councillor, 21" (Margaret). He wears coronation attire similar to his lady's. He wears an admiral's hat trimmed in gold and decorated with white plumes.

Maid of Honor: Lady Ann Coke, 18" (Maggie). Her silver bodice is decorated with sequins and pearls. She wears pearl earrings and a tiara.

Maid of Honor: Lady Mary Baillie-Hamilton, 18" (Winnie). Her gown has amber drops and green jewels on the bodice. She wears three bracelets and a gold tiara.

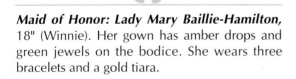

Maid of Honor: Lady Jane Heathcote-Drummond-Willoughby, 18" (Margaret). Her bodice is accented with diamond and ruby pendants. Her gold tiara is accented with rubies and diamonds.

Maid of Honor: Lady Rosemary Spencer-Churchill, 18" (Margaret). Her silver dress is accented on the bodice with pearls. Her tiara and earrings are made of pearls. She wears an aquamarine pendant.

Maid of Honor: Lady Jane Vane-Tempest-Stewart, 18" (Winnie). She wears a silver lamé dress with a bodice sprinkled with diamonds. Her jewels include rubies, diamonds, and aquamarines.

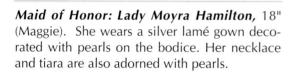

Maid of Honor: Lady Moyra Hamilton, 18" (Maggie). She wears a silver lamé gown decorated with pearls on the bodice. Her necklace and tiara are also adorned with pearls.

Queen during Investiture, 18" (Margaret). Her majesty wears a garment of linen under a golden cloak embroidered with symbols of the British Commonwealth.

Queen in Recessional, 18" (Margaret). The Queen is dressed in a coronation robe of purple velvet heavily trimmed in ermine. A gold chain with seven medals is draped around her shoulders.

Queen in Processional, 18" (Margaret). The Queen is dressed in a red velvet robe trimmed in ermine over a satin dress decorated in gold. She is dressed for the processional from Buckingham Palace to Westminster Abbey.

Queen Mother, 18" (Margaret). Her gown of white brocade is embroidered with jewels. Over the gown is a purple velvet robe trimmed in ermine.

Princess Margaret, 18" (Margaret). Her white gown adorned with jewels is worn under a purple velvet robe trimmed in ermine. She wears two diamond bracelets, earrings, necklace, and tiara.

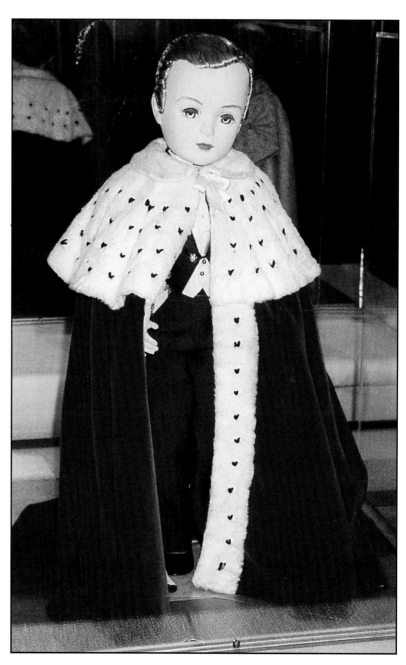

Prince Charles, 11" (Precious Toddler). Prince Charles wears linen pants and a silk shirt with lace at the collar and cuffs.

Duke of Edinburgh, 21" (Margaret). Prince Phillip wears a crimson velvet robe over his formal navy uniform.

Duke of Richmond, 21" (Margaret). He wears similar clothing as the Duke of Gordon. The Scepter with the dove pledges equal justice.

Marquis of Hastings, 21" (Margaret). He is dressed similarly in coronation attire. The Golden Spurs which represent chivalry and knighthood are carried on a red velvet cushion.

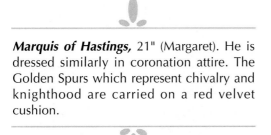

1954
Bible Characters

The Bible Characters were made in 1954 in very limited numbers. My research has been unable to determine the exact number of sets made. Eight Bible Characters were made and are considered to be the rarest of 8" dolls made by Madame Alexander. The eight dolls appeared in a black and white advertisement in Kansas City in 1954. Up until this set of dolls surfaced there was serious doubt that Queen Esther and Mary of Bethany had ever been put into production. Rhoda and Timothy had only been seen in prototypes. The Herald House Advertisement states: "These dolls were designed by Madame Alexander, world famous New York doll designer. Made of porcelain finished unbreakable plastic, they are authentically costumed, and even the dyes are matched to shades typical of Biblical times. Their eyes move, they walk, and their heads move from side to side as they move! Each doll is 7½" high and comes boxed with a small booklet telling the story played by the real character in the bible. In stock for immediate shipment."

The Bible Characters pictured are all straight leg walkers. A few of the Bible Characters have surfaced as straight leg nonwalkers. This set was found in the original boxes and had belonged to the original owner.

All have black pupiless eyes except for Queen Esther who has the very rare dark brown pupiless eyes. Background design by Ric Markin.

Queen Esther, Old Testament, Book of Esther. She has dark hair with dark brown pupiless eyes. Her taffeta undergarment is trimmed in gold. Her very elaborate robe of purple taffeta and gold leaf on white taffeta is accented with a belt of gold elastic.

A back view of *Queen Esther* shows her gold crown with a purple scarf attached. She wears simple, cotton panties and gold fuzzy-bottom shoes.

Rhoda, 8", *New Testament,* Acts 12:13-15. Her dress is of striped linen and closes with three tiny blue buttons down the back. She has a dark brown flip-style hairdo.

Side view of **Rhoda** shows her blue felt hat with a gold button covered in the center with blue felt on each side by her ears. Her lantern is attached to her wrist with a gold cord. The lantern is a gold cylinder with holes. A gold button on top and bottom complete the lantern.

Left: **Martha,** *New Testament,* Luke 10:38. Martha's red cotton dress is trimmed at the neck, sleeves, and hem with picot trim. She has dark hair with braids.

Right: Back view of **Martha** shows her headpiece of red and white flower trim on a navy band. The Star of David in the center is made of a one-piece plastic that looks like pearls. Her blue scarf is attached with red brads.

Martha with curls at each side instead of braids. She is mint with wrist tag. She won best of show in 8", at the 1999 M.A.D.C. convention.

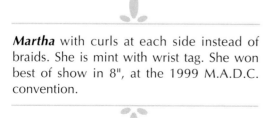

Mary of Bethany, *New Testament,* Luke 10:39. Mary wears a polished cotton dress with a green cotton overdress. Her dark brown hairdo is in the flip style. She won a best of show ribbon at the 1998 M.A.D.C. convention.

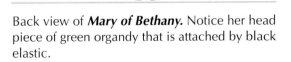

Back view of **Mary of Bethany.** Notice her head piece of green organdy that is attached by black elastic.

Timothy, *New Testament,* I & II Timothy. His short brown linen outfit is trimmed with fringe. He has a soft, curly brown wig. His underpants are white with picot trim.

Back view of **Timothy** shows his felt hat with a one-piece Star of David. The center is accented with a pearl.

Joseph, 8", *Old Testament,* Genesis 37:3. Joseph wears his coat of many colors made of red felt with felt scallops. His undergarment is blue and he wears a leather skirt that ties on the shoulder. He wears a dark red leather belt over the skirt.

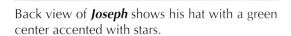

Back view of *Joseph* shows his hat with a green center accented with stars.

David, Old Testament, I & II Samuel. David has a soft, curly, red caracul wig and wears a band of braided cord. His faux fur is tied at the shoulder. His gold elastic belt snaps in back and is decorated with X brads. David is missing his harp.

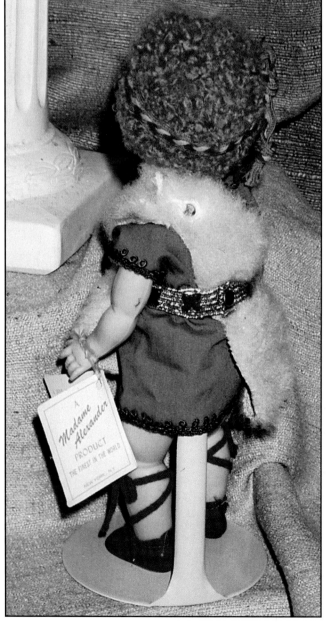

Back view of **David** shows his undergarment of deep rich green cotton with a bodice that has a snap in front. The bottom of the garment is a strip of material attached to the back of the bodice. It then comes between the legs, is twisted, and sewn to the front. Notice the strings on the shoes that crisscross and tie at the knee.

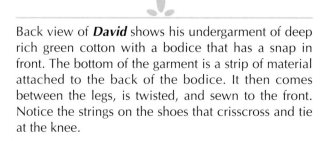

Ruth, Old Testament, Book of Ruth. Ruth's dress is navy blue with picot trim and is tied at the waist with a braid of red, yellow, and green. She carries a shaft of wheat.

Back view of **Ruth** shows her scarf attached to a gold band with stars. She wears black fuzzy-bottom shoes.

Pre-1980
Store Exclusives

Top of FAO Schwarz display box for 8" straight-leg walker **Wendy**.

 8", straight-leg walker **Wendy** in a display box with clothes and accessories. Notice the FAO Schwarz sleeve for the display box. FAO Schwarz Exclusive.

 Sleeping Beauty, 10". Dressed in a taffeta gown trimmed in gold. 1959 Disney exclusive.

 Wendy Ann, 8". Straight-leg non-walker. Mint and all original. Very rare. Made only in 1953.

Wendy Ballerina (#564), 8". Window box gift set with ***Guest for Luncheon*** (#542) and ***Coat, Hat, and Dress Set*** (#580). 1956 FAO Schwarz exclusive. Very rare.

Elise, 17". Dressed in a Godey-style outfit. Made for FAO Schwarz in 1962.

Katie and Tommy, 12" (Lissy). Exclusive for FAO Schwarz 100th Anniversary. 1962 only.

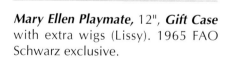

Mary Ellen Playmate, 12", ***Gift Case*** with extra wigs (Lissy). 1965 FAO Schwarz exclusive.

Pamela, 12", *Gift Case* (#1291) (Nancy Drew). Made for FAO Schwarz in 1965.

Alice and Her Party Kit, 14" (Mary Ann). Comes in a floral display box with extra wigs and clothes. Made exclusively for FAO Schwarz in 1965.

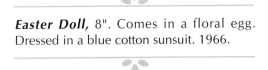

Easter Doll, 8". Comes in a floral egg. Dressed in a blue cotton sunsuit. 1966.

Cinderella, 14" (Mary Ann). Dressed in blue taffeta with gold trim. Made exclusively for FAO Schwarz in 1969.

Easter Doll, 8". Dressed in yellow polished cotton dress trimmed in lace with lace hat. Also made in 14" (limited to 300). 1968.

Sewing Basket, 8". Comes with four complete outfits that are ready to sew. Made for FAO Schwarz, 1966 – 69.

Left: **Snow White,** 14" (Mary Ann). Made only for Disney 1967 – 77.

Right: **Snow White,** 8". Can have bend knees (1972) or straight legs. Comes dressed in Disney crest colors. 1972 – 76.

Alice, 8". Can have bend knees (1972) or straight legs. Comes in blue cotton dress with white pinafore. 1972 – 76.

ABC Unlimited Productions

 Wendy Learns Her ABCs. 8", ABC Unlimited Productions. Wendy wears a blue jumper and beret. ABC blocks on skirt, optional wood block stand. Limited to 3,200. 1993.

Belk & Leggett Department Stores

Belk & Leggett is a department store chain based in the southeastern United States.

Miss Scarlett, 14" (Mary Ann). She is dressed in a green and white nylon voilé dress with green ribbon trim. Her dress tag says "Made for Belk Leggett — Miss Scarlett by Madame Alexander." 1988.

Rachel, 8". First in Southern Children Series. She is dressed in a ruffled lavender taffeta dress adorned with ribbon and lace. 1989.

Nancy Jean, 8". Second in Southern Children Series. She wears a yellow taffeta dress and carries a basket of pink flowers. 1990.

Fannie Elizabeth, 8". Third in Southern Children Series. She wears a pink cotton dress of pink and blue flowers, organdy pinafore, and a natural straw hat. Limited to 3,000. 1991.

Annabelle at Christmas, 8" (Cissette). Fourth in Southern Children Series. She wears a red plaid dress and holds a string of Christmas cards. Limited to 3,000. 1992.

Caroline, 8". Caroline wears a pink and white check cotton dress and is ready to catch a butterfly in her net. Limited to 3,600. 1993.

Holly, 8". She wears a white taffeta dress with red velvet bodice. Tiny gold bells, holly leaves, and berries adorn the neck and skirt. Unique hair style of a small braid encircles her face. 1994.

Elizabeth Belk Angel, 8". She is dressed in a white taffeta dress with an overskirt of red taffeta edged in gold. 1996.

Bloomingdales
Department Store

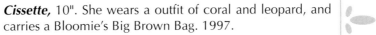

Cissette, 10". She wears a outfit of coral and leopard, and carries a Bloomie's Big Brown Bag. 1997.

Celia's Dolls

 David, the Little Rabbi, 8". He wears a rabbi outfit and carries his prayer book. Came in three hair colors. Limited to 3,600. 1991 – 1992.

Child at Heart

My Little Sweetheart, 8". Three hair colors. Limited to 4,500 dolls. 500 were African American. 1992.

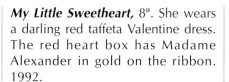

Easter Bunny, 8". She wears a pink gingham bunny outfit and carries a metal basket with eggs and chickens. (1500 blondes, 750 brunettes, 750 redheads.) Limited to 3,000. 1991.

My Little Sweetheart, 8". She wears a darling red taffeta Valentine dress. The red heart box has Madame Alexander in gold on the ribbon. 1992.

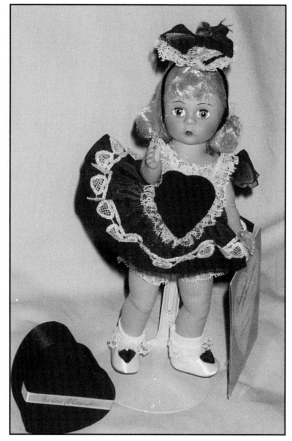

Trick and Treat, 8". Treat is dressed as a pumpkin and Trick as a black cat. Limited to 3,000 sets. 1993.

Trick and Treat, 8". 400 sets were sold with an African American Treat. 1993.

Childcraft

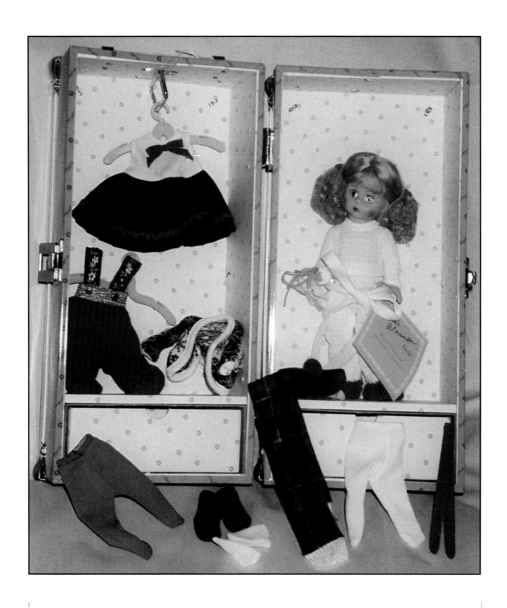

Wendy, 8", Winter Trunk Set. Wrist tag states "Specially Made for Childcraft." Outfit on doll is tagged "Wendy Loves." Alexander signature blue trunk. The doll and outfits are from the Winter Box Set in the 1994 line. 1994.

Christmas Shoppe

Alpine Boy and Girl, 8". Twins in Alpine Christmas outfits. Limited to 2,000 sets. 1992.

Collectors United Atlanta

Yugoslavia F.A.D., 8". She has a pearl headpiece, ribbon, handkerchief, and pink shoes added. Limited to 625. 1987.

Yugoslavia, 8". Doll on the left is from the regular Alexander line and the factory altered doll for the Collectors United is on the right.

Miss Leigh, 8". Named for the Green's oldest daughter, Leigh. She wears a yellow nylon dress over yellow taffeta and holds a white straw picture hat. Limited to 800. 1989.

Tippi, 8". All original for Collectors United. This is a replica of the costume Tippi Green wore in her performance of Swan Lake. It is a white satin and net ballet costume. Limited to 800. 1988.

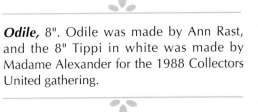

Odile, 8". Odile was made by Ann Rast, and the 8" Tippi in white was made by Madame Alexander for the 1988 Collectors United gathering.

Shea, 8". Named for the Green's youngest daughter, Shea. She wears a red felt jacket and skirt, green tights, brown felt hat, and elf slippers. Limited to 1,000. 1990.

Ring Master, 8". He is ready for his announcing job at the big top in his colorful jacket and top hat. Limited to 800. 1991.

Faith, 8". She wears a pink and white striped dress trimmed in lace. Her matching hat and basket complete the costume. Limited to 800. 1992.

Love, 8". She is dressed in an ecru dress adorned with lace and gold embroidery. A heart-shaped pocket is embroidered with "Love" on it. She wears a tiny pearl and lace hat. Limited to 2,400. 1994.

Hope, 8". She wears a 1900-style dress with hobble skirt and Gibson girl hairdo. She is ready for the Easter Parade with her elaborate straw hat. Limited to 900. 1993.

Alice in Wonderland Tea Party, a Collectors United souvenir. Alexander blue box contained Alice paper plates, napkins, and cups. 1991.

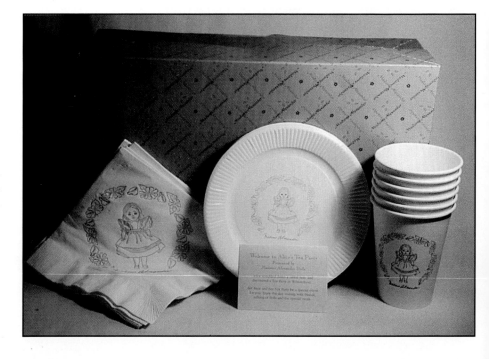

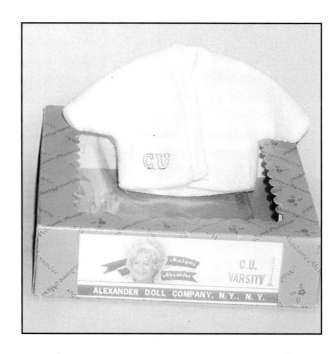

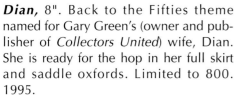

Dian, 8". Back to the Fifties theme named for Gary Green's (owner and publisher of *Collectors United*) wife, Dian. She is ready for the hop in her full skirt and saddle oxfords. Limited to 800. 1995.

Special Alexander event souvenir at Collectors United. C.U. Varsity sweater for an 8" doll.

1996 special event souvenir C.U. Olympics tote bag.

Olympia, 8". Made for the Collectors United gathering in honor of the Olympics held in Atlanta. Tagged "C.U. Goes To The Olympics." Limited to 800. 1996.

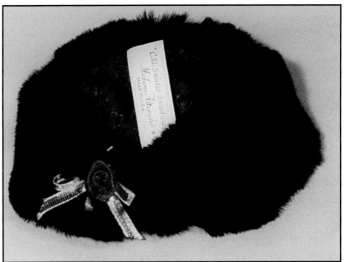

Left: 8", tagged "C.U. Salutes Broadway." She wears a gold bodice and burgundy skirt with a velvet jacket, and a gold necklace of tragedy and comedy masks. She carries a miniature playbill, ticket, and gold bag. Limited to 650. 1997.

Above: The special event souvenir is a black faux-fur cape lined in burgundy. Tagged same as 1997 doll.

Right: **Polynesian Princess,** 8". Her South Seas sarong and top are accented with a yellow flower. She has one long braid tied with a yellow ribbon. Limited to 600. 1998.

Left: This special event souvenir grass skirt with gold and colored bead accents also came with gold sandals. The necklace was a table favor. The skirt is not tagged. Limited to 600. 1996.

Above: **Fortune Teller,** 8". She wears a red print dress with purple velvet bodice and hat and comes with a crystal ball. 1999.

Right: Special Alexander event souvenir at 1999 Collectors United Gathering. Gold, red, and lavender scarves attach to the costume for the 8" doll. It also includes four bracelets.

Fortune Teller, 21". Her outfit includes a red print dress accented with gold rickrack and trim with a purple velvet bodice with gold coins draped at waist. She also wears a gold coin necklace. 1999.

Carnival Queen, 16" (Coco). This is a special event doll dressed in a pink or blue gown with an overskirt of white leaf and rose design lace, pearl earrings, and gloves. Limited to 24. 1999.

Majestic Midway, 21". This was a one-of-a-kind raffle at an Alexander event. She wears a spectacular gold costume. 1999.

Collectors United
Winter Wonderland
Nashville

Nashville Skater, 8". She was altered from the regular Alexander line altered by adding a black fur hat tied with a hot pink ribbon, matching muff, and black ice skates to make a Victorian skater. Limited to 200. 1991.

Nashville Skier, 8". Nashville Skier F.A.D. (right) was made from the regular line Tommy Tittlemouse (left) by adding hat, skis, and scarf. Limited to 200. 1992.

First Comes Love, 8". She comes with a bridal gown, rack, and bouquet. Her peach chemise is tagged and trimmed in lace and pearls. Limited to 200. 1993.

Nashville Goes Country, 8". Her western outfit is set off by her felt hat with sequins. She also comes with a guitar. 1995.

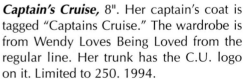

Captain's Cruise, 8". Her captain's coat is tagged "Captains Cruise." The wardrobe is from Wendy Loves Being Loved from the regular line. Her trunk has the C.U. logo on it. Limited to 250. 1994.

Sunny, 8". She wears a yellow rain coat and hat with black rain boots. Her dress has a white bodice and red print skirt. Limited to 300. 1996.

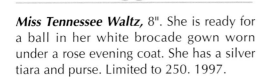

Miss Tennessee Waltz, 8". She is ready for a ball in her white brocade gown worn under a rose evening coat. She has a silver tiara and purse. Limited to 250. 1997.

C.U. Goes to Camp, 8" (Maggie). F.A.D. She is ready to play ball with her glove, bat, and bag. 1998.

Now I'm Nine, 8". This doll celebrates the 9th year of Nashville Winter Wonderland. She wears a blue party dress and carries a package. Limited to 300. 1999.

Other Collectors United Events

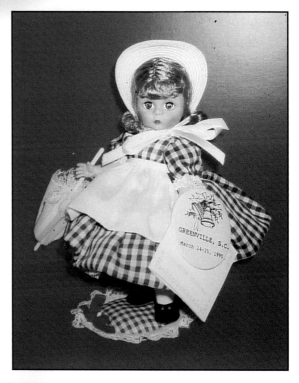

Bride of Tommy Snooks, 8". This is F.A.D. Bessy Brooks with added white straw hat, apron, and parasol. Box has gold seal marked "Greenville, S.C., March 24, 1990." Limited to 250. South Carolina event doll, 1990.

Greenville Halloween Special, 8". Left: This is Jumping Joan from the line. Right: This is a F.A.D. with witch's hat, trick or treat bag, and black mask. Also includes a cardboard black cat. Limited to 250. South Carolina event doll, 1990.

Left: ***Camelot in Columbia,*** 8". F.A.D. Maid Marion wears a tagged cape and a cone-shaped hat adorned with marabou. Limited to 400. South Carolina event doll, 1991.

Right: Back of ***Camelot in Columbia*** cape showing tag: "Camelot in Columbia."

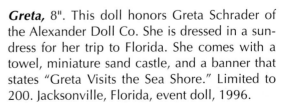

Greta, 8". This doll honors Greta Schrader of the Alexander Doll Co. She is dressed in a sundress for her trip to Florida. She comes with a towel, miniature sand castle, and a banner that states "Greta Visits the Sea Shore." Limited to 200. Jacksonville, Florida, event doll, 1996.

Collectors United
Doll Shop Exclusives

Cameo Lady, 10" (Cissette). She wears a Victorian costume, dainty bonnet, and parasol in white trimmed in black. Limited to 1,000.

Le Petit Boudoir, 10" (Cissette). F.A.D. Limited to 700. 1993.

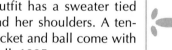

Physical Fitness, 8". Her tennis outfit has a sweater tied around her shoulders. A tennis racket and ball come with the doll. 1995.

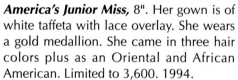

America's Junior Miss, 8". Her gown is of white taffeta with lace overlay. She wears a gold medallion. She came in three hair colors plus as an Oriental and African American. Limited to 3,600. 1994.

Judge's Interview, 8". She wears a perfect dress for an interview with the judges. Her small gold brooch has a red jewel in the center. Limited to 500. 1995.

Sailing with Sally, 8". Sally is wearing a white dress trimmed in pink. Her wooden sailboat is ready to go. 1998.

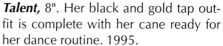

Talent, 8". Her black and gold tap outfit is complete with her cane ready for her dance routine. 1995.

Gary Green, 8". Alexander Doll Co. introduced this doll at Collectors United to honor Gary Green for his contributions to the world of Alexanders. He is the owner and publisher of *Collectors United* and host of C.U. Gatherings in the south. This doll completes the Green family in dolls. Visor cap reads "Collectors United" and comes with flowers and Alexander box. 1998.

61

One-of-a-Kind Walt Disney Auction Dolls

Christine from Phantom of the Opera, 21".
She is dressed in blue silk trimmed with
pearls, beads, and lace. Accessories include a
bouquet and porcelain mask. 1990.

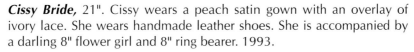

Cissy Bride, 21". Cissy wears a peach satin gown with an overlay of ivory lace. She wears handmade leather shoes. She is accompanied by a darling 8" flower girl and 8" ring bearer. 1993.

 Queen Guinevere, 21" (Margaret). She wears a royal dress of silk lace and embroidery. ***Sir Lancelot,*** 21". He wears a silk, brocade, and silver breastplate. Very exquisite dolls. 1995.

 Chess Set. Thirty-five dolls in sizes from 8" to 21" form the chess set on a satin chess board.

Cinderella, 10" (Cissette). She wears a blue satin gown tagged "Made Exclusively for Disney World Showcase of Dolls, Cinderella, by Madame Alexander." Limited to 250. From the First Annual Disney Showcase of Dolls, 1989.

Snow White, 12" (Nancy Drew). She wears a taffeta dress with net overlay and a cape accented with gold. Limited to 750. From the Second Annual Disney Showcase of Dolls, 1990.

Alice in Wonderland, 10" (Cissette). This doll is in the traditional Alice costume with white rabbit. Limited to 750. From the Third Annual Disney Showcase of Dolls, 1991.

Queen of Hearts, 10" (Cissette). She is very elegant in red and comes with a flamingo. Limited to 500. From the Fourth Annual Disney Showcase of Dolls, 1992.

Alice In Wonderland, 12" (Lissy). She wears a blue pique dress and organdy apron. Jabberwocky is made of green crushed velvet and looped fringe. Limited to 500. From the Fifth Annual Disney Showcase of Dolls, 1993.

Tweedledee and Tweedledum, 8". Alice finds this pair as she is trying to get out of the woods in *Through the Looking Glass.* They wear identical outfits with names on collars and hats with propellers. Limited to 750 sets. From the Sixth Annual Disney Showcase of Dolls, 1994.

Morgan LeFay, 10" (Cissette). She wears an elaborate costume trimmed in gold (King Arthur's half-sister from Camelot). Limited to 500. From the Seventh Annual Disney Showcase of Dolls, 1995.

Knave, 8". He wears a black velvet hood, red brocade pants, and a card with two of spades. (A Knave with different colors and five of spades was in the regular line.) Limited to 500. From the Eighth Annual Disney Showcase of Dolls, 1996.

Toto, 8". He wears a body of gray felt and a pink felt tongue is glued to his mouth. He comes in a wicker basket with a bouquet of flowers. Limited to 750. From the Ninth Annual Disney Showcase of Dolls, 1997.

Goldilocks and Baby Bear, 8". Goldilocks wears a blue and purple print dress. Baby Bear is made by Robert Raikes Collectibles. Limited to 350. From the Tenth Annual Disney Showcase of Dolls, 1998.

Disneyland Teddy and Doll Classic

Monique, 8". She wears a lavendar moiré taffeta dress with lace trim. Limited to 250. From the Disneyland Teddy Bear and Doll Classic, 1993.

Annette, 14". Sculpted by Robert Tonner and produced by the Alexander Doll Co., Annette wears the classic Mousketeer outfit. Limited to 400. From the Disneyland Teddy Bear and Doll Classic, 1993.

Disney Store Exclusives

Bobby Soxer, 8". She wears a classic 1950s costume with a poodle skirt, angora sweater, and wears a class ring around her neck. 1990.

Mousketeer, 8" (Maggie). She wears the original Mousketeer costume. Her hair is pulled to the back of her neck and tied with a blue bow. 1991.

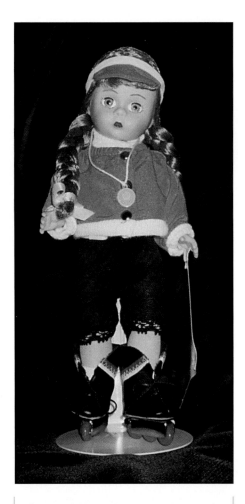

Thoroughly Modern Wendy, 8". She wears roller blades, a sun visor, and is ready for a day of fun. 1992.

Round-Up Cowgirl, 8". She wears a western outfit worn by Mousketeers on the *Mickey Mouse Club.* 1992.

Snow White, 10" (Cissette). She wears the Disney crest colors. 1993.

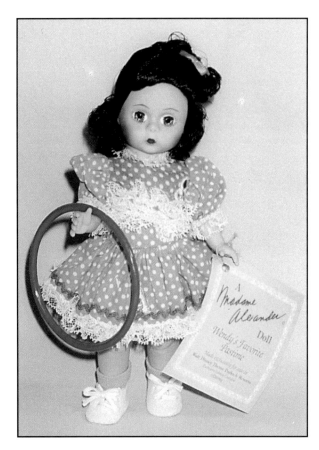

Wendy's Favorite Pastime, 8". She comes with a hula-hoop and wears a pink and blue polka dot outfit with a pink "A" on the front of the skirt. 1994.

Belle, 8". She is dressed in a yellow ballgown from the Disney version of *Beauty and the Beast.* 1994.

Blue Fairy Tree Topper, 10" (Cissette). She wears a long chiffon gown of blue and carries a gold star-tipped wand. 1995.

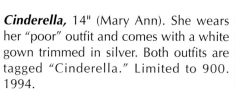

Cinderella, 14" (Mary Ann). She wears her "poor" outfit and comes with a white gown trimmed in silver. Both outfits are tagged "Cinderella." Limited to 900. 1994.

Sleeping Beauty, 14" (Mary Ann). She is wearing a peasant dress and comes with a satin gown. Both outfits are tagged "Sleeping Beauty." 1995.

Cinderella, 14" (Mary Ann). She is dressed in the pink gown made by the mice for the palace ball. She also comes with the white satin ballgown tagged: "Cinderella." 1995.

Cinderella, 14" (Mary Ann). She is dressed in the white satin ballgown that her Fairy Godmother created for the ball. The gown is trimmed in silver crystals. Tagged: "Cinderella." This outfit is the only one that is included with the pink ballgown.1995.

Belle, 14" (Mary Ann). She is dressed in the blue cotton town dress, white blouse, and apron from *Beauty and The Beast.* Catalog exclusive.

Mary Poppins, 10" (Cissette), 1996.

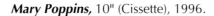

Dolls and Ducks Doll Shop

 Ice Princess, 8". She wears a sparkly silver costume accented at the waist with a blue ribbon and blue flower and a silver tiara with a blue jewel. Limited to 300.

Doll and Teddy Bear Expo

Shadow of Madame, 8". She wears a blue taffeta gown with an overlay of lace. She is a miniature of the 21" Madame in the 1989 line. Limited to 500. From the First Annual Doll and Teddy Bear Expo East,1994.

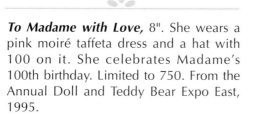

To Madame with Love, 8". She wears a pink moiré taffeta dress and a hat with 100 on it. She celebrates Madame's 100th birthday. Limited to 750. From the Annual Doll and Teddy Bear Expo East, 1995.

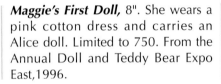

Maggie's First Doll, 8". She wears a pink cotton dress and carries an Alice doll. Limited to 750. From the Annual Doll and Teddy Bear Expo East, 1996.

Love Is in the Air, 8". She is wearing a bride's outfit with a Peter Pan collar trimmed with pearls at the neckline and a pink rose. Limited to 100. From the Annual Doll and Teddy Bear Expo West, 1999.

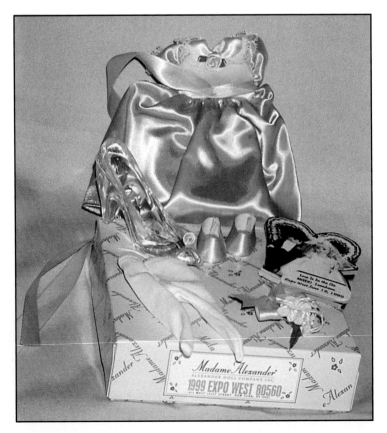

Bridesmaid (outfit only). Pink satin dress with Peter Pan collar, white pantyhose, pink shoes, and bouquet. Limited to 100. From the First MADC Luncheon at Doll and Teddy Bear Expo West. 1999.

Holiday Magic, 8". She is ready for the holidays in her gold and red gown. From the Doll and Teddy Bear Expo East, 1999.

Eliza Doolittle, 21". She is a vision in a white lace dress and parasol with her upswept hairdo and charming hat. From the Doll and Teddy Bear Expo One-of-a-Kind Auction,1996.

One of a Kind
Madame Alexander
21" Eliza Doolittle
Designed by Daun Fallon

Dolls 'n Bearland
of Scottsdale, Arizona

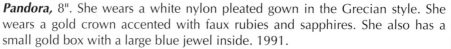

Pandora, 8". She wears a white nylon pleated gown in the Grecian style. She wears a gold crown accented with faux rubies and sapphires. She also has a small gold box with a large blue jewel inside. 1991.

Dolly Dears

Bo Peep, 8". This doll from Alexander line has a staff and is accompanied by two Dakin sheep. 1987.

Susannah Clogger, 8" (Maggie). She wears her clogging outfit complete with taps on her shoes. An all original doll. Limited to 400. 1992.

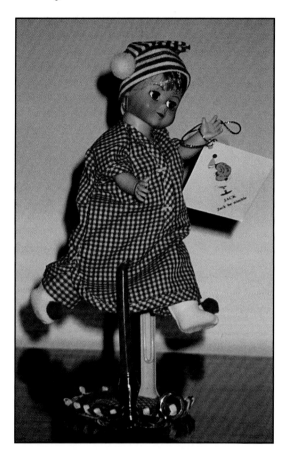

Jack Be Nimble, 8". He is a factory re-dressed doll from Jack who was discontinued from the regular line in 1992. He came with a brass candlestick, red candle, Ann Rast stand, and original Jack outfit. Limited to 288. 1993.

Princess and the Pea, 8". She wears an elegant blue gown of faille trimmed in lace and silver accents and her brocade Juliet cap is trimmed in pearls. Limited to 100. 1993.

Mattress for the Princess and the Pea. The paisley covered mattress came in a separate blue box. 1993.

Elegant Dolls and Toys

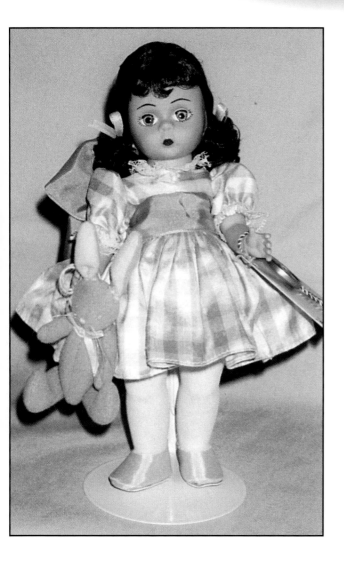

Elegant Easter, 8". She is dressed in a pink checked silk taffeta dress and comes with a brown velvet bunny. Limited to 300. 1998.

Heart of Dixie, 8". She is dressed in a red velvet and lace gown. Limited to 289. 1998.

Enchanted Doll House

Enchanted Doll, 8". She wears pink check and was made in the image of the logo of the Enchanted Doll House. Limited to 3,000. 1980.

Enchanted Doll, 8". She was re-issued after first doll sold out immediately. Eyelet was used on the pinafore instead of lace. Limited to 3,423. 1991.

Blue Ballerina, 8". This doll came with the Enchanted Doll House trunk. The trunk came with extra clothes not made by Alexander. 1983 – 85.

Blue Ballerina (box #430), 8". The Blue Ballerina was only available at Enchanted Doll House in 1989. Limited to 360. 1989.

25th Anniversary, 10" (Cissette). She is a blue-eyed brunette doll dressed in a pink and white gingham and lace dress and wears a silver logo Enchanted Doll House pendant around her neck. Limited to 5,000. 1988.

Farmer's Daughter, 8". She comes with a hoe and almanac. Limited to 4,000. 1991.

Vermont Maiden, 8". This is the official 1991 Bicentennial doll with pottery jug stating "Vermont 1791 – 1991." Limited to 3,600. 1991.

Farmer's Daughter Goes to Town, 8". A cape and basket were added and re-issued as Farmer's Daughter Goes to Town. Limited to 1,600. 1992.

FAO Schwarz

Brooke, 14" (Mary Ann). She wears a red polka dot dress and white pinafore with the FAO Schwarz logo on the pocket. She came with a Steiff posable bear and was available in blonde or brunette. 1988.

David and Diana, 8" twins. They came with their own wooden wagon. (Named for Princess Diana and an executive at FAO Schwarz.) They are packaged in one box with the wagon. 1989.

Me and My Scaasi, 21" (Cissy). (Which was last produced in 1960) was designed by Arnold Scaasi. The tulle ballgown is sprinkled with faux ruby jewels. 1990.

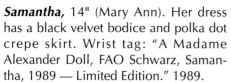

Samantha, 14" (Mary Ann). Her dress has a black velvet bodice and polka dot crepe skirt. Wrist tag: "A Madame Alexander Doll, FAO Schwarz, Samantha, 1989 — Limited Edition." 1989.

Sailor, 8". He is in a traditional sailor's outfit with the FAO Schwarz logo on his hat. 1991.

Beddy Bye Brooke, 14" (Mary Ann). She wears a cotton nightie under a red velour robe and carries a FAO Schwarz clock tower ornament. Beddy Bye Brenda wears an identical outfit. Sold as a set.

Beddy Bye Brenda, 8". Notice the FAO Schwarz logo on the red ribbons. 1991.

Carnavale Doll, 14". Her dress is a harlequin design in black and white satin. She carries a silver mask. 1991 – 92.

Wendy Shops FAO, 8". She wears a stylish outfit of polished cotton set off by her straw hat. She is ready to go with her purse, FAO shopping bag, and piano keyboard. 1993.

The Secret Garden, 8" trunk set. She is portraying Mary Lennox in a Victorian navy and black dress. She also wears a black felt hat with upturned brim. She carries a key and has a basket with a robin. 1994.

Enchanted Princess, 8". She comes with Frog Princess, Cinderella, and Sleeping Beauty outfits in a signature trunk. 1995.

Left: ***Lucy Ricardo,*** 8". Lucy's 1950s dress is accented with a black patent belt and purse. Limited to 1,200. 1995.

Below: ***I Love Lucy,*** 8". Fred, Ethel, Lucy, and Ricky were sold as a set. 1995.

Fun with Dick and Jane, 8". The clothes are from the original story *Fun with Little Quack.* They come with a miniature book and vinyl duck. Limited to 1,200 sets. 1995.

The Little Rascals, 8". Alfalfa, Darla, Spanky, Buckwheat, and dog Petey are from the *Our Gang* comedy. Unusual Alfalfa is 8" doll with 10" legs. Limited to 2,000 sets. 1996.

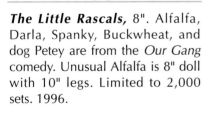

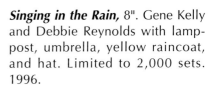

Singing in the Rain, 8". Gene Kelly and Debbie Reynolds with lamp-post, umbrella, yellow raincoat, and hat. Limited to 2,000 sets. 1996.

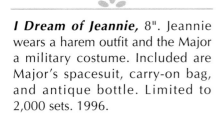

I Dream of Jeannie, 8". Jeannie wears a harem outfit and the Major a military costume. Included are Major's spacesuit, carry-on bag, and antique bottle. Limited to 2,000 sets. 1996.

Lucy and Ethel, 8". Dressed for working in the chocolate factory, Lucy wears a pearl necklace while Ethel has a pearl bracelet. Also included is a small bag of chocolates. Limited to 2,500 sets. 1997.

Honeymooners Set, 8". This tribute to the 1950s comedy series includes Ralph, Alice, Trixie, and Norton. Ralph wears his bus driving suit. The set comes with a telephone, coffee pot, and whisk. Limited to 2,000 set. 1997.

Grease, 10" (Cissette). Danny and Sandy are dressed in black leather motorcycle jackets. Made for the 20th Anniversary of the release of *Grease,* the movie. 1998.

Fay Wray, 10". With 20" King Kong by Steiff. Fay Wray all in white with bead and pearl accents is the damsel in distress. King Kong is made of mohair. Limited to 500 sets. 1998.

First Modern Doll Club of New York

Autumn in New York, 10" (Cissette). F.A.D. Limited to 260. 1991.

Left: Altered doll with fur-trimmed black cape and fur hat, white muff, and skates. Tagged: "First Modern Doll Club Luncheon."
Right: ***Gibson Girl*** in the Alexander line.

 Blue Angel, 8". She wears a dark blue and gold dress, halo, and resin wings. Tagged: "Blue Angel." Limited to 3,000. 1997.

Horchow

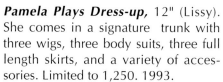

Pamela Plays Dress-up, 12" (Lissy). She comes in a signature trunk with three wigs, three body suits, three full length skirts, and a variety of accessories. Limited to 1,250. 1993.

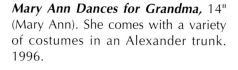

Mary Ann Dances for Grandma, 14" (Mary Ann). She comes with a variety of costumes in an Alexander trunk. 1996.

J. Magnin
Department Stores

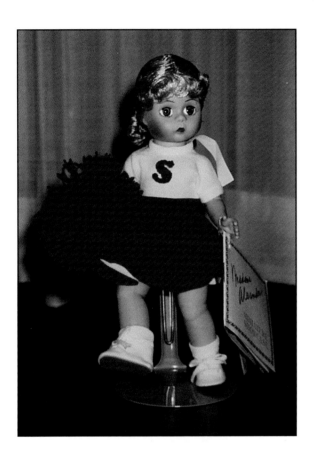

Cheerleader, 8". F.A.D. She is the same as in 1990 line except has an "S" on her blouse rather than an "A." Printed on end of box: "I.Magnin Special — 1990."

Miss Magnin, 10" (Cissette). She wears a pink crepe Chanel-type suit and carries a black purse and an I. Magnin hat box. Limited to 2,500. 1991 – 1993.

Little Miss Magnin, 8". With her tea set and teddy bear, Miss Magnin is ready for a party. Limited to 3,600. 1992.

Bon Voyage Miss Magnin, 10". Her steamer trunk and navy and white fitted dress with a perky hat are perfect for a trip. Limited to 2,500. 1993.

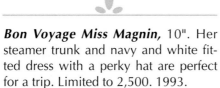

Bon Voyage Little Miss Magnin, 8". She comes with a cute sailor dress, teddy bear, and suitcase. Limited to 3,500. 1993.

Little Miss Magnin Supports the Arts, 8". With her pink painter smock with a red ribbon for Aids Awareness plus her teddy bear and paints, she's ready for anything. 1994.

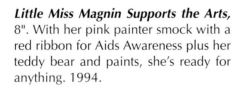

Jacobson's

Wendy Starts Her Collection, 8". She comes with a 3" bear. Her dress has a pink brocade bodice and taffeta skirt with an overlay of lace. Limited to 2,400. 1994.

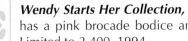
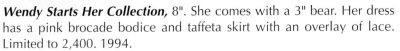

Jean's Doll Shop

Wendy Walks Her Dog, 8". To complete this, the jacket was changed and the dog was added to Her First Day of School. F.A.D. Limited to 500 pieces. 1995.

Lillian Vernon

 Home For the Holidays, 8". She wears a green and gold holly print dress and carries a small gold package. 1996.

Madame Alexander Doll Club Convention Dolls

Fairy Godmother, 8". First M.A.D.C. convention souvenir is a non-Alexander doll company outfit made by Judy LaManna with convention book. 1983.

Above: **Ballerina,** 8". This F.A.D. has a ribbon stating "Madame Alexander Doll Convention 1984" attached to the tutu with an Austrian crystal. 1984.

Left: **Ballerina,** 8". She came as a blonde or brunette. 1984.

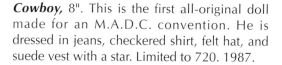

Scarlett, 8". Scarlett from the Alexander line has the green ribbon changed to red. Limited to 625. 1986.

Happy Birthday Madame. This F.A.D. is Mary, Mary from the Alexander line with the apron embroidered "Happy Birthday Madame." She comes with a small gift for the Madame. Limited to 450. 1985.

Cowboy, 8". This is the first all-original doll made for an M.A.D.C. convention. He is dressed in jeans, checkered shirt, felt hat, and suede vest with a star. Limited to 720. 1987.

Flappers. The white and red flappers are from the Alexander line. The 10" in the black outfit is the 1988 convention doll.

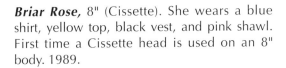

Flapper, 10". She wears a black fringed dress with rhinestones. She also wears pearls, a white headband, and rhinestone trimmed shoes. Limited to 720. 1988.

Briar Rose, 8" (Cissette). She wears a blue shirt, yellow top, black vest, and pink shawl. First time a Cissette head is used on an 8" body. 1989.

Queen Charlotte, 10" (Cissette). She wears an exquisite court gown of the late eighteenth century. A velvet cape trimmed in fur completes her outfit (not pictured). Her throne chair was a banquet centerpiece. Limited to 900. 1991.

Riverboat Queen, 8". Lena wears black lace over pink taffeta dress with a gold and diamond brooch at the neck. Limited to 900. Eighth convention, 1990.

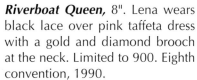

Prom Queen, 8" (Maggie). She is dressed in pale pink organdy trimmed in satin ribbon. Her fur wrap and gold tiara complete her costume. Limited to 1,100. 1992.

Navajo Woman, 8". Her top is dark green velvet and she wears three skirts which was common for women of the tribe. The top skirt is red calico, then a blue and purple skirt, and last a gold skirt. Limited to 835. 1994.

Diamond Lil, 10" (Cissette). Named for Lillian Russell of vaudeville fame. She is dressed in black velvet with faux diamond accents. She wears a straw hat and diamond necklace and earrings. The convention theme was Days Gone By. Limited to 876. 1993.

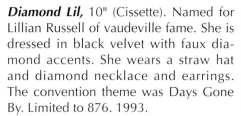

Frances Folsom, 10" (Cissette). The wedding gown is made of ivory faille which is a close replica of the gown Frances wore when she married President Grover Cleveland. A cathedral length veil is held in place by tiny flowers. 1995.

Las Vegas Showgirl. They came with a variety of haircolors and feather colors. Attendees received either a pink, blue, green, lavender, or white showgirl. Twenty lucky winners received showgirls with black feathers. 1996.

Las Vegas Showgirl, 10" (Cissette). She is attired in a gold body suit and headpiece adorned with feathers. Tagged: "Las Vegas Showgirl." 1996.

A robe for the Las Vegas Showgirl was a brunch souvenir. The terry robe has Madame Alexander on the back and came in a blue box.

Rose Festival Queen, 8". She rules over the Rose Festival in Portland, Oregon. She is elegantly attired in a white gown. Her cape has red velvet roses entwined around it. 1998.

A Little Bit Country, 8". This redhead in a western outfit holds a silver hand-held microphone. Tagged: "A Little Bit Country." Attendees also received a guitar in a black case. 1997.

Orange Blossom, 10" (Cissette). Her long gown is trimmed with lace at the neckline. Her hat is tied with a satin ribbon. Limited to 800. 1999.

Madame Alexander
Doll Club Dolls

Wendy, 8". First M.A.D.C. Club Doll wears a blue taffeta dress with a pink organdy pinafore. Wrist tag: "Wendy — MADC 1989 Club Doll, 1989 Exclusive Limited Edition."

Polly Pigtails, 8" (Maggie). She wears a white dotted swiss apron over yellow taffeta. She wears a miniature of the club logo around her neck. 1990.

Miss Liberty, 10" (Cissette). She wears a striped satin dress and velvet jacket with a star on the ribbon around her neck. 1991.

Little Miss Godey, 8". She wears a taffeta gown with a bustle and a tiny cameo at her neck. She carries a small beaded reticule. 1992.

Left: ***Wendy Loves Being Best Friends*** is in a pink taffeta dress and organdy pinafore. 1993.

Right: ***Wendy's Best Friend Maggie*** wears a blue taffeta dress and organdy pinafore. 1994. The double doll stand from M.A.D.C. has a table, two copies of *Shopper*, and a mini Alexander box.

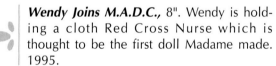

Wendy Joins M.A.D.C., 8". Wendy is holding a cloth Red Cross Nurse which is thought to be the first doll Madame made. 1995.

Wendy Honors Margaret Winson, 8" (Maggie). This doll honors Margaret Winson, M.A.D.C. founder. She wears a postal uniform because Margaret works for the post office. She carries a bag embroidered with "M.A.D.C. Mail." A dog is attached to her skirt. 1996.

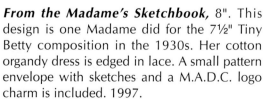

From the Madame's Sketchbook, 8". This design is one Madame did for the 7½" Tiny Betty composition in the 1930s. Her cotton organdy dress is edged in lace. A small pattern envelope with sketches and a M.A.D.C. logo charm is included. 1997.

Skate with Wendy, 8". She wears a cotton blouse, red vest, plaid capri pants, and comes with a skate key. Limited to 1,500. 1998.

Electra, 8". She wears a silver costume trimmed in pink and blue. Concept and design by Joe Carrillo. She is ready for the year 2000. Limited to 800. 1999.

Madame Alexander
Premiere Dolls

Sunshine Symposium, 8". She was created for the get together at Disney World and came with a basket with soap in the shape of peaches. (Not made by Alexander Doll Co.) 1985.

Wendy Goes to Disney World, 8". Made by Dorothy Starling for the Florida symposium. (Not made by Alexander Doll Co.) Limited to 100. 1986.

1987 Snowflake Symposium. Held in Schaumburg, Illinois. The souvenir outfit was made by Mary Voight. (Not made by Alexander Doll Co.) 1987.

1988 Snowflake Symposium, 8". She wears a gold and white dress created by Pamela Martenec. (Not made by Alexander Doll Co.) 1988.

1989 Snowflake Symposium. Red velvet skating outfit was made by Joan Dixon. (Not made by Alexander Doll Co.)

1990 Snowflake Symposium, 8". The theme was Winter Wedding and each person received a bridal outfit. (Not made by Alexander Doll Co.) 1990.

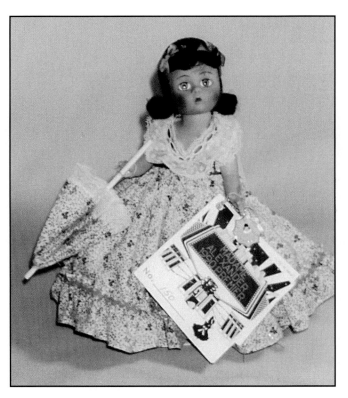

Scarlett, 8". The first premiere was held in Arlington, Texas. F.A.D. Scarlett has a different print from the line, green bows in her hair instead of a hat, and a parasol. Dress tag: "Madame Alexander Doll Club 1990 Scarlett." Limited to 800. 1990.

Springtime, 8". She wears lavender print on white dress with a cotton pinafore. The wooden cart and shovel were table favors at the Texas premiere. She is the first totally original doll made by Alexander Doll Company exclusively for premieres. Limited to 1,600. 1991.

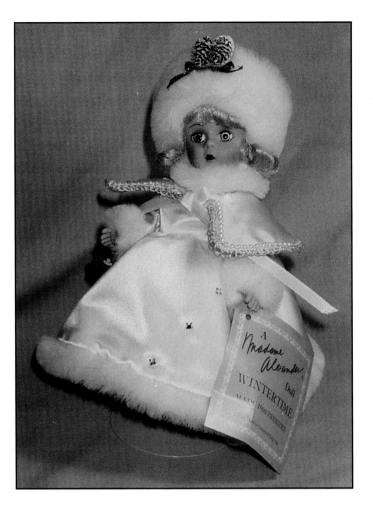

Wintertime, 8". This white satin outfit is trimmed in fur with fur hat with pine cone accents. The premieres were held at six locations throughout the country. Limited to 1,650. 1992.

Homecoming, 8". Under her stadium coat is a one-piece outfit of red and white tweed sweater and denim jeans with M.A.D.C. in red on her back pocket. A stadium blanket and pennant also were made by Alexander Doll Co. for her. Limited to 1,800. 1993.

Setting Sail for Summer, 8". Her tam and dress are of cotton with a red anchor print and are accented by red ribbons held by a gold star brad. Tag: "Wendy Loves Her Summer Cruise, etc." Limited to 1,800. 1994.

Snowflake, 8". Her skating dress is of gold tissue lamé. Her hat is made of fur with a gold snowflake in the center. She holds gold snowflakes between her hands. The premieres were held at six locations. Limited to 1,200. 1995.

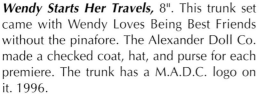

Wendy Starts Her Travels, 8". This trunk set came with Wendy Loves Being Best Friends without the pinafore. The Alexander Doll Co. made a checked coat, hat, and purse for each premiere. The trunk has a M.A.D.C. logo on it. 1996.

Boo, 8". F.A.D. From the 1996 Chicago symposium, Maggie wears a Halloween ghost costume over Mothers Day from the regular line. The robe is tagged "Boo." Limited to 150.

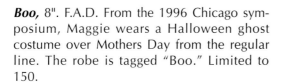

Wendy's Tea Party, 8". She wears a pink cotton organdy dress with a wide ribbon sash. A box set of accessories included a straw hat, lace purse, and gloves. Three premieres were held across the country. 1997.

Diamond Pixie, 8". She wears a red pixie costume and holds her star wand. Her special hairdo is braids brought to the top of the head with a ribbon holding them in place. Premieres were held in three locations. 1998.

Starlett Glamour, 10" (Cissette). Theme: Broadway on Tour. She is ready for a Broadway show in her black evening gown adorned with roses. She is wearing pearl earrings, bracelet, and necklace. Limited to 700. 1998.

Friends Around the Country was made for the 12 Friendship Luncheons across the country. Dress and pinafore tagged: "M.A.D.C. Friends Around the Country." Bag and hat were Texas luncheon souvenirs. Limited to 800. 1997.

Wendy Plays Masquerade, 8". Her butterfly costume is perfect for a masquerade party. Only the outfit was made and tagged by the Alexander Doll Co. Limited to 1,000. 1998 Friendship Luncheon.

Madame Alexander Doll Club
Travel Doll Party

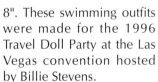

8". These swimming outfits were made for the 1996 Travel Doll Party at the Las Vegas convention hosted by Billie Stevens.

1999 Travel Doll Party came with brown boots, hat, and socks. Jewelry and canteen were party favors. Tagged: "M.A.D.C. 99." Limited to 430.

This Wendy Goes to the Fair outfit and garment bag were made exclusively for the 1997 Travel Party. Tagged: "Madame Alexander." Limited to 500.

Madame Alexander
Event Dolls and Items

Anastasia, 14". She wears a peach gown with blue puff sleeves and a duel hat of gold. Limited to 489. 1993.

This shoe bag of blue print with four pockets comes with white skates, bunny slippers, velvet evening shoes, and pink elastic sandals. Tag: "Madame Alexander Made in U.S.A." 1997 Nashville Convention.

M.A.D.C. 1991 tea sets were used as centerpieces at the welcome breakfast. They were made in West Germany by the Reutter Co. The small tea sets were a convention favor. Limited to 90 large sets.

Drucilla, 14". Cinderella's step-sister wears a gold accented gown. She was sold at the 1992 M.A.D.C. Convention. Limited to 268.

1886 Flower Girl, 8". She wears an ivory moire taffeta dress trimmed in pink rosette braid and lace. She carries a bouquet of flowers. The flowers in the lace basket were a table favor. 1995 M.A.D.C. companion doll.

Wendy Tours the Factory, 8" (Maggie). She wears a pink and blue print dress with organdy pinafore with Madame Alexander Tour Guide on front. Made for the 1996 Premiere attendees in New Jersey.

Bobby Takes a Picture, 8"
(Maggie). He wears a sailor
top and hat with blue plaid
shorts. He was made for the
1996 San Jose premiere only.
He has his camera ready to
take a picture. Limited to 215.

Cheshire Cat, 8". A Cheshire Cat in
pink colors instead of maroon was
issued for the Alexander line. His
face is painted with a wide grin and
whiskers and he is from *Alice In
Wonderland*. Limited to 215. Made
in maroon for the 1996 M.A.D.C.
premiere only. Made in 1997 in pink
for the regular Alexander line.

Margaret O'Brien. She was made to coincide
with Miss O'Brien's presence at the Portland
convention. Her cotton dress and pinafore is
accented with her straw hat. 1998 Portland
M.A.D.C. convention companion doll.

Left: ***Alice and White Rabbit***. These dolls are from the 1996 Alexander line. Alice has a blue banner stating "1996 Texas." She also comes with a looking glass mirror, a gold key, a timepiece on a gold chain added by the premiere, and her "pig" baby. 1996 centerpiece at the Texas premiere.

Below: ***Alice's Pig Baby***. The Pig Baby is from Germany and is wearing a lace bonnet made by Linda Crowsey. The blanket is tagged "Madame Alexander" and was made by the Alexander Doll Co.

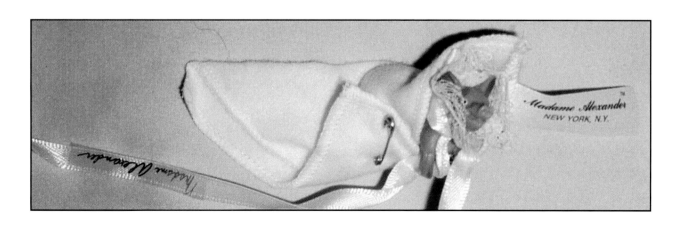

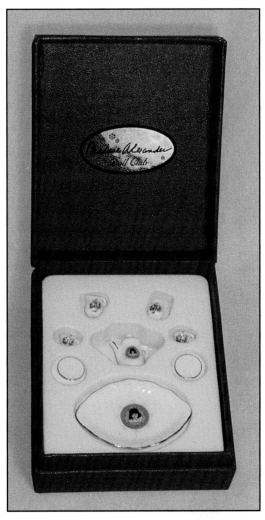

Maggie Visits Rockefeller Center, 8" (Maggie face). She wears a white leotard, red velvet skirt, knitted scarf, hat, and red skates. A limited edition doll made available to club members. Limited to 350. 1998.

Right: Large tea set made by Reutter exclusively for 1997 premiere centerpieces.

Above: Small tea set made exclusively for 1997 premiere attendees by Reutter.

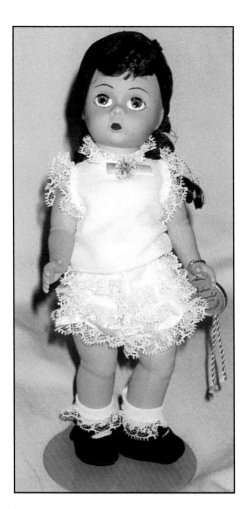

Undergarment Doll, 8". She comes in a variety of hair colors. Tagged: "Wendy's M.A.D.C. Boutique." She is in her cute chemise and ready for club members to dress.

Springtime Darling, 8". She wears a sparkly blue dress over white eyelet. A special limited edition doll sold only to club members. Limited to 350. 1999.

Wendy Loves the Dionnes. Raffle item for the 1994 Phoenix Convention made by the Madame Alexander Doll Co. for the 60th birthday of the Dionnes. The five, one-of-a-kind, 8" dolls are dressed in cotton batiste dresses in pastel colors. They came in a basket.

Cissy Showgirl. She wears a golden, jeweled costume with pink marabou and feathers. Her headpiece of gold and feathers is very dramatic. She is a one-of-a-kind made for the raffle at the 1996 Las Vegas Convention.

Orange Blossom. This one-of-a-kind African American doll was made for the 1999 M.A.D.C. convention auction. It is identical to the convention doll except it's African American.

Lilly Pulitzer, 21" (Cissy). She wears a flowered dress with a matching bag with a swimsuit enclosed. She's from the Breakfast Event at the 1999 M.A.D.C. Convention. Limited to 25.

Event Dolls
Not made by
Madame Alexander

Teddy Bear Picnic was made by Jean Stanton. 1988 M.A.D.C. El Paso dinner.

Teddy bear and basket that was made for 1988 El Paso Teddy Bear Picnic.

Irish Leprechaun, outfit for 8" doll. Theme Irish Springtime. He comes with shamrock and shillelagh. Made by Gay Stewart and Jean Stanton for the 3rd El Paso M.A.D.C. dinner. 1990.

8" Mexican Girl outfit. Pre-convention souvenir. Boy outfit could be purchased separately. 1987.

The Yellow Rose of Texas outfit was given to hostesses and used as the brunch centerpiece. Made for the 1987 convention.

Davy Crockett, a brunch souvenir of real leather by Rebba Sutherland, was made for the 1987 convention in San Antonio.

Davy Crockett Girl outfit. 1987.

This Breyer horse comes with blanket, bed roll, and M.A.D.C. medallion at neck. Souvenir for the 1987 convention.

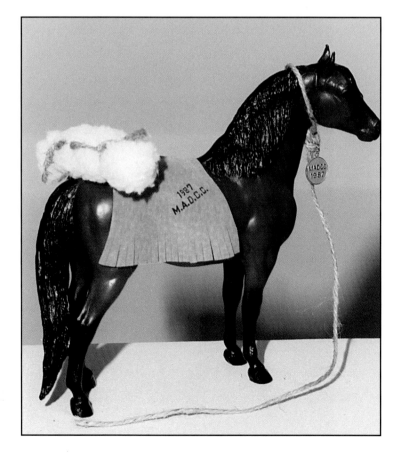

This Poodle with leash was given at a 10+ event at the 1988 Chicago convention. It was to go with the **Flapper**.

Poor Cinderella outfit for an 8" doll was designed by Judy Hernandez. M.A.D.C. All-In-A-Row Event at the 1989 convention.

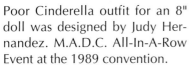

This Alice in Wonderland outfit was made by Alice Toovey and Pat Burns. It was a 5+ event souvenir at the 1989 M.A.D.C. convention.

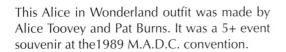

This Tinkerbell outfit was a 10+ event souvenir at the 1989 M.A.D.C. convention. It was tagged: "Tink M.A.D.C.C. 10 plus, 1989."

This Pirate outfit outfit was made by Barbara De Mille. It was a 10+ event souvenir at the 1990 M.A.D.C. convention.

Page with Crown. He was made to go with the throne centerpiece for Queen Charlotte at the 1991 M.A.D.C. convention.

Children's Event souvenir for the 1991
M.A.D.C. convention.

Perfect 10 Luncheon. Souvenirs for
M.A.D.C. members who had attended all
ten conventions. 1992 M.A.D.C. convention in Chicago.

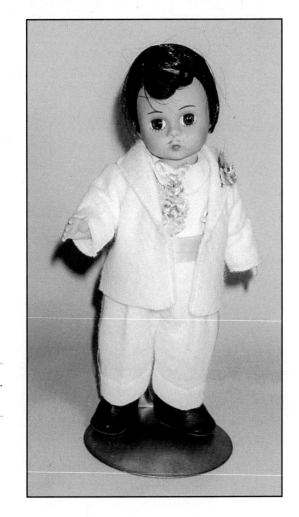

Prom Queen's Date. From the 1992 M.A.D.C.
convention in Chicago.

Centerpiece doll made for the 1992 Texas Premiere Banquet.

Maid. She was a centerpiece doll from the 1993 M.A.D.C. convention.

This was a centerpiece at the 1992 Chicago M.A.D.C. convention.

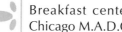

Breakfast centerpiece at the 1992 Chicago M.A.D.C. convention.

Event souvenir outfit for the 1993 M.A.D.C. 5+ luncheon.

Ten plus centerpiece and souvenir outfit from the 1992 Chicago M.A.D.C. convention.

Outfit and buggy were souvenirs at the 10+ luncheon for the 1993 M.A.D.C. convention.

Centerpiece doll from 1994 Texas Premiere. Her purple velvet costume is trimmed in gold sequins. Made by Lucy Whisenant.

Twenty plus souvenir outfit at the 1997 Nashville M.A.D.C. convention. The outfit was made by Dorothy Starling.

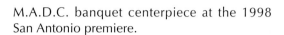

M.A.D.C. banquet centerpiece at the 1998 San Antonio premiere.

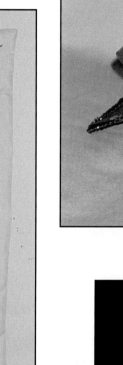

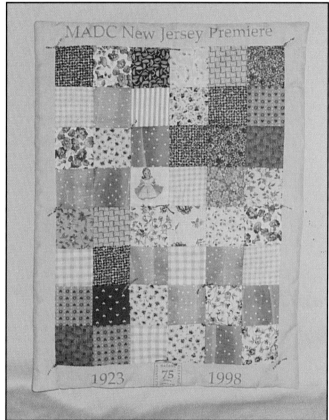

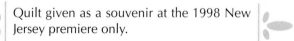

Quilt given as a souvenir at the 1998 New Jersey premiere only.

Banquet centerpiece at the 1999 M.A.D.C. Orlando convention. The outfit was made by Joan Dixon.

Madame Alexander Doll Company

Mid-year Releases

 Welcome Home. This mid-year special in honor of the Desert Storm soldiers came in white and African American boys or girls. 1991.

Wendy Loves Being Loved, 8". This doll comes with a wardrobe in a window box. 1991.

Queen Elizabeth II, 8". This mid-year special was in honor of 40th anniversary of coronation. 1992.

Rumpelstiltskin and the Miller's Daughter, 14". The Miller's Daughter comes with a spinning wheel and 8" Rumpelstiltskin. Limited to 3,000 sets. 1992 only.

Christopher Columbus, 8". He is dressed in brown velvet trimmed in gold and carries a map. Made for the 500th anniversary of the discovery of the New World. 1992 only.

Queen Isabella, 8". This mid-year release doll commemorates the 500th anniversary of the discovery of the New World. She wears a dark green velvet gown trimmed in gold. 1992 only.

Wendy Honors Madame, 8". She is dressed in a pink satin gown as a miniature of the 21" Madame made in 1984. 1993.

Scarlett O'Hara, 8". This mid-year release doll is a re-creation of the 1937 Scarlett outfit. In honor of the 70th anniversary of the Alexander Doll Co. 1993.

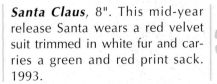

Santa Claus, 8". This mid-year release Santa wears a red velvet suit trimmed in white fur and carries a green and red print sack. 1993.

Mrs. Claus, 8" (Maggie). This mid-year release doll wears a long, red velvet dress trimmed in fur and a festive red and green print apron and mop cap. 1993.

Wicked Witch of the West, 8". This mid-year release doll wears a black and red costume and has a pointed felt hat. She carries her colorful broom. 1994.

Wizard of Oz, 8". This mid-year release Oz wears his magical green metallic outfit with a black top hat over a fluffy white wig. 1994.

Dorothy, 8". In her Emerald City outfit, Dorothy wears a green plaid jumper with a white top, green socks, and red sequin shoes. She also carries a wicker basket with Toto. Mid-year release. 1994.

This 8" doll was created as a special doll for events or retailers, with a sash denoting the organization. She wears a lacy organza dress with a pink satin ribbon at the waist. The dress is tagged "A Special Event Doll, 1994."

Wendy Ann, 8". She is dressed in a copy of a 1950s outfit. She is one of the Madame Alexander's 100th Anniversary Collection honoring the life of Madame Alexander (1895 – 1990). 1995.

Wendy Salutes the Olympics, 8". Alexander Doll Company made this beauty in 1996 in honor of the Olympics for their platinum dealers.

Sir Lancelot du Lac, 8". This mid-year release is an outstanding doll in blue and maroon with his sword and crown decorated with jewels. 1995.

Queen Guinevere, 8". She is dressed splendidly in court attire and a crown of gold with jewels. Mid-year release. 1995.

Maggie Mix Up, 8" (Maggie). This is a post office commemorative in blue gingham. A postcard with a stamp is with Maggie. 1997.

George and Martha Washington, 8". They are dressed in period costumes trimmed in gold and pearls. Limited to 1,500 sets. 1998.

75th Anniversary Wendy. In honor of the anniversary, she is dressed in a frilly pink dress and comes with an Alexander box. 1998.

Special event or store doll in 1996. Store or event was printed on the hat box.

Wendy's Special Cheer. Alexander Doll Company special doll for events or stores in 1998. The sweater was embroidered with the store or event. This one was for FAO Schwarz.

Limited Editions

An American Legend. Outside of display box that contains Madame doll, hard cover book, and back drop. Limited to 1,500. 1999.

An American Legend, 10" (Cissette). She is dressed as Madame in 1923, and comes with a backdrop of the first location of the company and a hard-cover book. Limited to 1,500. 1999.

Melody and Friend, 24". Melody is a porcelain doll and her friend is 8" Wendy. They are both dressed in pink and white striped silk and organdy pinafores designed by Hildegard Gunzel. Limited to 1,000 sets. 1992.

Courtney and Friends, 25". Courtney and her friends, an 8" boy and girl, were designed by Hildegard Gunzel. Limited to 1,200 sets. 1993.

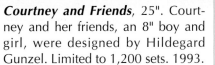

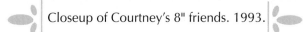
Closeup of Courtney's 8" friends. 1993.

Marshall Field

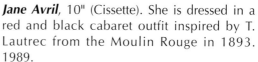

Jane Avril, 10" (Cissette). She is dressed in a red and black cabaret outfit inspired by T. Lautrec from the Moulin Rouge in 1893. 1989.

Madame Butterfly, 10" (Cissette). She is dressed in a brocade underdress and gold obi and has Oriental facial features. She is tagged: "Marshall Field's Exclusive — 1990 Madame Butterfly."

Metroplex
Doll Club

 Spring Break, 8". Factory re-dressed doll. Towel and skirt tagged "Spring Break." Umbrella and chair were table favors at Metroplex Banquet. Limited to 400. 1992.

My Doll House

Above left: **Southern Belle**, 10". Her pink satin gown is tagged "My Doll House, Southern Belle, by Madame Alexander." Her pink parasol and picture hat complete the ensemble. Limited to 2,300. 1989.

Above right: **Queen Elizabeth I**, 10". She wears a velvet dress with brocade sleeves. Dress is tagged "My Doll House, Queen Elizabeth I." Limited to 2,400. 1990.

Left: **Empress Elizabeth of Austria**, 10" (Cissette). She wears a gold and ecru illusion over satin gown and a faux diamond crown. Limited to 3,600. 1991.

Neiman Marcus

Miss St. John, 21". She is in a chic wool suit with matching hat and comes with a brief-case. Her jewelry consists of gold earrings, a bracelet, a necklace, and pin. Limited to 750. 1998.

Party Trunk, 8". The doll comes with signature Alexander trunk and four outfits that are tagged, but not tagged Neiman Marcus. Limited to 1,044. 1990.

Anne Series for Neiman Marcus, 8". A character from Lucy Maud Montgomery books. She wears her puff sleeve burgundy satin dress. She also comes with a nightie and print cotton travel bag all in an Alexander signature trunk. 1994.

Caroline's Storyland Trunk. This trunk contains Bo Peep, Blue Fairy, and Alice outfits. The red dress with apron is tagged "Made exclusively for NM/Caroline by Madame Alexander."

Noel, 12". First Madame Alexander porcelain Christmas doll. Red velvet dress not tagged. Box: "Madame Alexander First Porcelain Christmas Doll." Limited to 5,000. 1989.

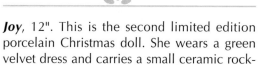

Joy, 12". This is the second limited edition porcelain Christmas doll. She wears a green velvet dress and carries a small ceramic rocking horse. Limited to 5,000. 1990.

Summer Cherry Picking. She wears a cherry print dress with red checked trim and red checked panties. She also wears red side snap shoes. Limited to 500. 1998.

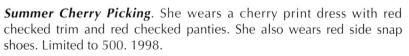

Betsy Ross, 8". A very patriotic costume of red, white, and blue. Limited to 500. 1998.

Home for the Holidays, 10". She wears a red and gold overskirt and a green taffeta skirt. Comes with a small card that states "My Darling I'll Be Home for Christmas – Your Beloved." Limited to 400. 1998.

Pilgrim Girl, 8". She is ready for Thanksgiving in a long blue dress with leaf embossed collar and apron. Comes with a miniature pumpkin. Limited to 500. 1998.

A Rose for You, 8". A lovely lace trimmed dress with a rose decoration at the neck and a red rose for a gift. 1998.

Pollyanna, 8" (Maggie). Dressed in a blue checked cotton dress with tiny pearl buttons down the front of the bodice. Natural straw hat with flowers and blue checked trim. Limited to 500. 1999.

Lavender Rose, 10" (Cissette). Dressed in a lavender satin fitted gown with a billowing overskirt. 1999.

Blossom, 8". Dressed in a pink cotton print with script in gold and pink satin sash. Comes with bouquet of flowers. Limited to 500. 1999.

Little Bo Peep, 8". Dressed in a pink gown trimmed in lace. Comes with her staff and a lace hat. Limited to 700. 1999.

Investigator Wendy, 8". Dressed in a red print dress with checked coat and Sherlock Holmes-type hat. Comes with a spy glass. Limited to 500. 1999.

Saks Fifth Avenue

Sak's Own Christmas Carol, 8". Her tartan plaid taffeta skirt and sleeves are set off by a black velvet bodice. Available in three hair-colors and African American. 1993.

Joy, the Joy of Christmas, 1994, 8". Dressed in a forest green taffeta dress with ruffled pan-niers. A green bow and small red rosette adorn the center of the waist. Two hair colors — blond and brunette.

Shirley's Doll House

 Angel Face, 8" (Maggie). She is wearing a blue gown sprinkled with gold. Store addition of a gold harp. Limited to 3,500. 1990.

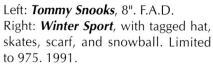

Left: ***Tommy Snooks***, 8". F.A.D.
Right: ***Winter Sport***, with tagged hat, skates, scarf, and snowball. Limited to 975. 1991.

 Tagged hat from Winter Sport. 1991.

Wendy Visits the World Fair, 8" . Wendy in her 1893 lace outfit to honor the 100th anniversary of the Chicago World Fair. Limited to 3,600. 1993.

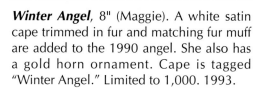

Winter Angel, 8" (Maggie). A white satin cape trimmed in fur and matching fur muff are added to the 1990 angel. She also has a gold horn ornament. Cape is tagged "Winter Angel." Limited to 1,000. 1993.

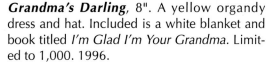

Grandma's Darling, 8". A yellow organdy dress and hat. Included is a white blanket and book titled *I'm Glad I'm Your Grandma*. Limited to 1,000. 1996.

Maypole Dance, 8". She wears an organdy dress and pinafore re-created from the 1950s. The doll was produced in three hair colors plus an African American version. The doll commemorates 20 years of Shirley's Dollhouse. Limited to 3,000. 1994.

Shriner's 1st Ladies' Luncheon

Texas Shriner, 8". Our little Shriner wears a fez hat, jeans, shirt, and vest with a Texas star on the back. Limited to 1,800. Made for the 1993 Shriner's Convention in San Antonio.

Spiegel's

 Beth, 10" (Cissette). Beth of *Little Women* in a period 1865 costume of pink brocade trimmed in lace. Dress tag: "Made Exclusively for Spiegel's, Beth by Madame Alexander." 1990.

Merry Angel, 8". A Christmas tree topper in shimmering gold and red velvet. 1991.

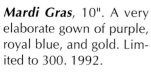

Mardi Gras, 10". A very elaborate gown of purple, royal blue, and gold. Limited to 300. 1992.

United Federation of Doll Clubs (U.F.D.C.)

Sailor, 8". Dressed in a turn-of-the-century sailor outfit made of gray gabardine. Theme: Children of Washington. Limited to 260. 1990.

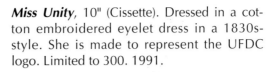

Miss Unity, 10" (Cissette). Dressed in a cotton embroidered eyelet dress in a 1830s-style. She is made to represent the UFDC logo. Limited to 300. 1991.

Little Emperor, 8". Dressed in an elaborate silk costume trimmed in gold. Limited to 400. 1992.

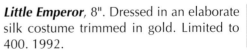

Columbian Sailor, 12" (Lissy). Dressed in black velvet pants, red velvet jacket, and hat in honor of the 1893 Columbian Exposition. Limited to 380. 1993.

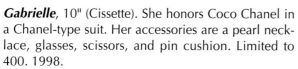

Gabrielle, 10" (Cissette). She honors Coco Chanel in a Chanel-type suit. Her accessories are a pearl necklace, glasses, scissors, and pin cushion. Limited to 400. 1998.

U.F.D.C. Mannequin, 8". A gift from the Alexander Doll Company to each guest. The hard plastic mannequin is draped with a tape measure ribbon and fabric. It came in an Alexander box. Limited to 400. 1998.

Price Guide

1953 CORONATION SET (Pages 7 – 20) . . . . .N.P.A.

1954 BIBLE CHARACTERS (Pages 21 – 28) .$7,000.00 ea.

PRE-1980 STORE EXCLUSIVES (Pages 29 – 24)
Wendy in display box $3,000.00
Wendy Ann $3,500.00
1956 Window box gift set $3,000.00
Sleeping Beauty $375.00
Elise $2,000.00
Katie and Tommy . . . .$1,800.00 pair
Mary Ellen Playmate Gift Case $1,200.00
Pamela Gift Case $900.00
Alice and Her Party Kit $750.00
Easter Doll (in egg) $1,500.00
Cinderella $425.00
Easter Doll (yellow outfit) $1.200.00
Sewing Basket $950.00
14" Snow White $350.00
8" Snow White $425.00
8" Alice $450.00

ABC UNLIMITED PRODUCTIONS (Page 35)
Wendy Learns Her ABCs $125.00

BELK & LEGGETT DEPARTMENT STORES (Pages 36 – 38)
Miss Scarlett $150.00
Rachel $75.00
Nancy Jean $75.00
Fannie Elizabeth $85.00
Annabelle at Christmas $125.00
Caroline $100.00
Holly $100.00
Elizabeth Belk Angel $100.00

BLOOMINGDALES DEPARTMENT STORE (Page 39)
Cissette $105.00

CELIA'S DOLLS (Page 40)
David, the Little Rabbi $75.00

CHILD AT HEART (Pages 41 – 42)
Easter Bunny $350.00
My Little Sweetheart $75.00

Trick and Treat . . . .$190.00 set

CHILDCRAFT (Page 43)
Winter Trunk Set $150.00

CHRISTMAS SHOPPE (Page 44)
Alpine Boy and Girl . . . .$185.00 set

COLLECTORS UNITED (Pages 45 – 52)
(Atlanta)
Yugoslavia F.A.D. $100.00
Tippi $425.00
Miss Leigh $150.00
Odile $125.00
Shea $175.00
Ring Master $125.00
Faith $250.00
Love $100.00
Hope $175.00
Alice in Wonderland Tea Party Set . . .$40.00
Dian $150.00
C.U. Varsity sweater $50.00
Olympia $150.00
C.U. Olympics tote bag $50.00
C.U. Salutes Broadway $175.00
Black faux-fur stole $50.00
Polynesian Princess $175.00
Grass skirt $50.00
Fortune Teller, 8" $175.00
Fortune Teller accessories $50.00
Fortune Teller, 21" $600.00
Carnival Queen $300.00
Majestic Midway . . . . .N.P.A.

COLLECTORS UNITED WINTER WONDERLAND – NASHVILLE (Pages 53 – 56)
Nashville Skater $175.00
Nashville Skier $100.00
First Comes Love $250.00
Nashville Goes Country $150.00
Captain's Cruise $200.00
Sunny $200.00
Miss Tennessee Waltz $175.00
C.U. Goes to Camp $150.00

Index